Perfect Partners

A comedy

Alan Richardson

Samuel French — London
New York - Hollywood - Toronto

ISBN 0 573 12197 4

Please see page iv for further copyright information

CHARACTERS

Edwina, proprietor of "Perfect Partners"
Jonathan, her marital and business partner
David Murray, a visitor
Susan Carter, another visitor

CHARACTER NOTES

Edwina She is in her late forties or early fifties and is unhappy about it, trying desperately but unsuccessfully to pass for younger. She attempts to talk in a refined voice, but, at moments of stress, her local accent tends to surface. Her manner varies between being patronizing and razor-sharp.

Jonathan He is in the same age-bracket as Edwina. He has let himself well and truly go to seed and is often in a state of composed inebriation. He has a fondness for colourful vocabulary and imitation Shakespeare, and enjoys irritating people.

David Murray He is an earnest but diffident man in his twenties or early thirties. His appearance is tidy, unassuming and rather uninspiring.

Susan Carter She is a strikingly attractive girl in her twenties. She is fashionable, natural and pleasantly mannered.

Perfect Partners won the John Scott Salver at the SCDA One-Act Festival for original plays, and the Geoffrey Whitworth Trophy at the British Final.

PERFECT PARTNERS

The office of "Perfect Partners", a less than reputable introduction agency

There is one entrance from a hallway outside. The main item of furniture is an old desk. It is littered with papers and files. Hiding amongst the debris is an old-style telephone, a well-fingered index card file and a cheap-looking portable cassette recorder. There is one chair behind the desk, another two nearby, and a large overflowing wastepaper bin. A battered filing cabinet stands against one wall. On the walls are a number of wedding photographs. Scattered everywhere are old newspapers, plastic cups, unwashed milk bottles, etc. Unopened mail lies behind the door. Overall, the appearance could be summed up in one word: shabby

As the CURTAIN *rises, the telephone is ringing persistently. A key rattles in the lock of the door and a strained female voice is heard off*

Edwina (*off*) I hear you! I'm coming!

The phone continues to ring

Hang on, will you!

The door opens slowly and Edwina struggles in. She is encumbered with two plastic carrier bags of supermarket groceries and hasn't a free hand to answer the phone

Give us a bloody chance! I've only got two hands! (*She attempts to deposit one of the bags on the desk, but only succeeds in spilling part of the contents*) For crying out loud!

The phone unsympathetically persists

Hold your bloody horses! (*She finally extricates a free hand and snatches up the phone. In a split second, harassment is superseded by poised composure*) Good-afternoon. Perfect Partners, the friendly, caring introduction agency. Edwina Lovelock speaking. How may I assist you? (*She listens for a few seconds, then her face drops*) Oh, it's you again, Mr Harris. What's the problem this time?... Not happy about your last introduction. ... I see. (*She listens with little interest and begins checking her various purchases against the checkout slip. She throws in the occasional "Yes" or "I see" to suggest that she is actually listening, but this is momentarily forgotten when she is outraged by the price increase on an item*) Seven pence up in one week — bloody swindle! (*Into the phone*) What? ... Sorry, just my little comment on inflation. ... Yes. Well, I'm sorry the evening wasn't a stunning success. I do sympathize. ... Of course I do! ... Look, Mr Harris, shall we be candid? ... Good. I think people ought to be candid. I do agree we seem to be having the teensiest problems finding your perfect partner. But it is a question of finding a young lady to match your specific requirements. (*She takes a card from the index file*) Ah, yes, here we are. Now correct me if I err, but you did insist on a young lady about twenty-five, slim, blonde? Yes. ... Yes of course we have such ladies on our books. ... Why haven't you met one yet? Well, here's where we have to be terribly candid. There honestly aren't too many slim, twenty-five year old blondes desperately keen to meet fifty-three year old, balding, beer-bellied bricklayers. ... I beg your pardon? ... And you! (*She slams the phone down*) Moron! What do you expect for fifty quid? (*She tears up the card and drops the pieces in the wastepaper bin. She returns to her shopping*)

The door opens and Jonathan, her estranged husband, enters. He has obviously had more than a few drinks

It's you! To what do I owe this honour?
Jonathan Just visiting, my darling. Just visiting.
Edwina Where were you when I needed you?
Jonathan You still have need of me? I'm flattered.

Edwina Don't be! I meant at the supermarket. I had to cart all this myself.

Jonathan Abject apologies. Completely slipped my mind. Still, as long as you remembered the essentials. (*He searches inside the carrier bags*)

Edwina You needn't bother looking. I don't need to keep you in booze any more, thankfully.

Jonathan Thoughtful as always, my darling. What will I do without you? (*He opens the filing cabinet and finds a half-finished bottle of whisky. During the following, he finds a used plastic cup, tips out the contents, cleans the inside with his fingers and pours in some whisky*)

Edwina You'll find out soon. So where were you?

Jonathan Business lunch.

Edwina Liquid lunch, you mean.

Jonathan Both. Simply discussing a little business proposition with some friends.

Edwina Your boozy pals. And another white elephant that'll cost us.

Jonathan Us? I'm a free agent now ... almost.

Edwina Not yet. Until all the papers are signed, we're still legally husband and wife. You're not blowing any more money until we've settled maintenance, so forget it..

Jonathan (*toasting her*) And I still adore you, too. You will have your pound of flesh. I'm letting you keep the business.

Edwina (*looking around*) Thanks a million.

Jonathan By the way, are you planning to change the name after I'm gone? "Perfect Partners" sounds a bit inappropriate. Doesn't seem right any more.

Edwina Was it ever for us?

Jonathan Once ... I thought.

Edwina Upon a time ... long ago.

But their moment of retrospection is shrilly interrupted by the phone

Damn! If that's another complaint, I'll tell them to stick it up their ... (*Answering the phone, instantly posh*) Afternoon. Perfect Partners, the friendly, sincere introduction agency. Edwina Lovelock at your service. ... Oh, hallo, Mr Sinclair. How nice to hear from you. ... (*Aside to Jonathan*) Owns three petrol stations. Loaded. (*Back to phone*) Did you? Jolly good. And how did the evening go? ... It didn't? ... Oh dear. ... Yes. ... Yes. ... It is all down to good old chemistry. What did she dislike? ... I see. Well, not everybody cares for pipe smoke. I don't know why. I think a pipe makes a man look sort of — rugged. What else? ... Your choice of music. ... Which is? ... Ah. ... Personally, I'm positively turned on by the Black Dyke Mills Band, but, "one person's meat" — as they say. Not to worry. Let's see if we can find you someone more sophisticated. I'll just get one of my staff to program your data through our KN five-o-five digital computer. (*She switches on the portable cassette recorder and the sound of sundry whirls, bleeps and clicks is heard. During this, she thumbs her way through the card file*) Here we are. (*She selects a card and switches off the cassette recorder*) Direct from the computer print-out. Oh, yes. I couldn't have chosen better myself. A perfect match, I'd say. ... Did I? Well, if at first you don't succeed. ... What? ... At seventeenth? ... Oh, very witty.

Jonathan (*examining the card*) No! You couldn't? Not soggy Sarah? How many years have you been trying to get rid of her?

Edwina (*to Jonathan*) Not so loud!

Jonathan The face that sank a thousand ships — and she's got that neurotic Afghan hound.

Edwina (*to Jonathan*) Belt up! (*On the phone*) Sorry. Just disciplining one of my junior staff. Yes, of course. I'll forward you her details first post. By the way, you don't mind pets, do you? ...No? Good. And you won't forget the additional ten pounds? Just to cover administration. Good. Cheery-bye. (*She replaces the phone*) Another satisfied sucker. That's how it's done.

Jonathan Had I a hat, I'd take it off to you.

Edwina Spare me the banter. If you're going to hang around here, make yourself useful.

Jonathan Name the task.

Edwina I haven't looked at the mail. See if there's anything worth bothering about.

Jonathan Why not? One last time for nostalgia's sake. (*He scoops up the mail and starts opening letters*)

Edwina begins sorting out her groceries

Phone bill — the red one.

Edwina Bin.

Jonathan And a complaint.

Edwina Ditto.

Jonathan Now this sounds more promising. (*Reading*) "Dear Perfect Partners, You nearly got it right this time. We both liked opera. We both liked tennis. We both liked Chinese food. The only thing we didn't like was each other." (*He drops the letter in the bin*) Ditto.

Edwina Nobody paying yet?

Jonathan Not so far. Another complaint. Calls us — "fraudulent charlatans".

Edwina Bloody nerve!

Jonathan I don't know. Sounds quite classy — "fraudulent charlatans". And she wants her fifty quid back.

Edwina Fat chance! This isn't a charity.

This letter is also consigned to the bin

Jonathan And, last but not least, a completed application form.

Edwina And fifty quid! (*She snatches the cheque that is attached to the form*) OK. I'd better do the normal re-write. That'll be the usual candidate for the Booker prize for fiction. (*She gets a blank application form from the filing cabinet*) Right. Fire ahead. Name?

Jonathan (*reading*) "Mizz Olivia Gardener" — as in green fingers.

Edwina (*writing*) Miss Olivia Gardener. Address?

Jonathan "Seven Montego Terrace".

Edwina Worth a bob or two. Age?

Jonathan "Young thirties".

Edwina Thirty-nine and a half. Status?

Jonathan "Single".

Edwina Eternal optimist. Occupation?

Jonathan "Community Relations Consultant".

Edwina Social worker. Describe your appearance?

Jonathan "Homely".

Edwina Back end of a bus.

Jonathan And "cuddly".

Edwina Overweight. Interests?

Jonathan Quite a list. Starting with "occasional theatre".

Edwina Went on staff Christmas outing to last year's pantomime.

Jonathan "Keep fit. Jogging. Callanetics. Green issues. The environment. Nuclear disarmament. Pollution. Animal rights" ——

Edwina Hold it! Hold it! Let's condense that. (*She writes*) Everything that's currently "in". Describe your ideal perfect partner?

Jonathan "Healthy. Active. Handsome. Professional. Solvent. Caring. Generous".

Edwina Meal ticket. Right. I'll fill in the minor details later.

Jonathan Have we got any environmentally aware company directors who jog around nuclear power stations?

Edwina Dozens! What do you think? We'll start her off with a few from the bottom-of-the-barrel file.

Jonathan (*pouring himself another drink*) Plenty of those. Sure I can't tempt you?

Edwina No. And don't think you're going to sit there getting sloshed. I've got work to do.

Jonathan Don't mind me. My sole object is total inebriation.

Edwina Then go back to your pals at the boozer. After all, it is your second home.

Jonathan Soon be my only home.

Edwina Don't get maudlin! Besides, you can always move in with your little tart.

Jonathan That would suit you, my darling. Then your half-wit toyboy wouldn't have to keep one eye on his watch.

Edwina Half-wit? It takes one to know one.

There is a soft knock on the door which goes unheard in the argument

Jonathan At least my "little tart" doesn't have a headache three hundred and sixty-four nights of the year!

Edwina At least my "toyboy" lasts longer than a TV commercial!

The knock is repeated, louder this time

What was that?

Jonathan I think a visitor calls.

Edwina Who the hell ...

Jonathan You are up to date with the rent?

Edwina Shut it! And keep it that way. (*She opens the door*)

David Murray is standing outside. He hesitates self-consciously

(*Snapping*) Yes?

David Sorry to disturb, but I was looking for the premises of "Perfect Partners".

Jonathan You've found us.

David I wasn't sure. But I knew someone was here when I heard ... voices.

Edwina So?

David I was hoping perhaps for an interview.

Edwina Sorry. We usually contact our clients by post or phone.

Jonathan (*whispering in her ear*) Fifty quid!

Edwina But we can make an exception in your case, Mr ——?

David Murray. David Murray.

Edwina Do come in, Mr Murray. Take a pew.

David Thank you. (*He comes into the room and sits down*)

Edwina Welcome to "Perfect Partners". Edwina Lovelock, proprietrix, at your service. And this is my dearest spouse, Jonathan.

Jonathan Delighted to make your acquintance.

Edwina I do apologize for the designer debris. This is just a temporary bivouac while our usual suite of offices are being redecorated.

Jonathan And the staff are in Ibiza on an all expenses paid holiday.

Edwina (*throwing Jonathan a dirty look*) Do tell me, David — you don't mind? Informality is our keyword — how did you find out about our agency?

David I heard about it from others.

Edwina Personal recommendation?

David Not exactly. To be honest, you don't know the real reason I'm here.

Edwina But I think I do, David. You see, overcoming your understandable reluctance to approach a professional matchmaker is the first big step towards finding your perfect partner. (*Getting into her sales* *pitch*) We live in a constantly changing society where go-ahead, dynamic young people like yourself find it increasingly difficult to make meaningful contact with the opposite sex.

Jonathan I blame it all on the demise of the good old dance halls. In my younger days, many's the time I used to pick up ——

Edwina Yes, the discos have definitely killed romance.

David The noise certainly kills conversation.

Jonathan Reduces communication to animal grunts and gestures.

Edwina A subject my dear husband is expert on.

David Sorry?

Edwina Studying. His Open University course.

David I see.

Edwina (*whipping out an application form*) So, to business. I'll just take down your particulars.

Jonathan As the actress said to the bishop.

Forced laughter all round

Edwina Now, you know why you're here. And I know why you're here.

David Don't be too sure of that

Edwina Of course I am. Now, David, the sooner we know all about you, the sooner we'll be able to find your perfect partner.

David You're confident you can do that?

Edwina Indubitably. Why, amongst the hundreds of names in our extensive files, there must be that certain someone just waiting for you.

David Hundreds?

Edwina At my very fingertips. (*She shows him the card file*) There you are, from A to Z.

David (*looking through the file*) I see. You seem to have a lot under "S".

Jonathan That's all the Smiths.

David Ah. But I am puzzled.

Edwina Do tell.

David If you're so good at finding everybody's perfect partner, why have you got hundreds left?

Edwina New clients like yourself joining every day. And perhaps some slightly unrealistic requirements. You can't please all of the people ... Shall we begin? Your name we already have. Address?

David Twelve Hillpark Avenue.

Edwina Would that be private?

David Council.

Edwina (*her disappointment undisguised*) Never mind. Age? — and it does pay to be honest.

David Twenty-seven.

Edwina Status?

David Single.

Edwina Still flying solo. Describe your appearance? (*She looks at him*) Don't bother — (*hastily*) I mean, I'm sure you can trust me on that bit — with a hint of flattery thrown in. Interests?

David Nothing special. Ten-pin bowling. Watching TV. Occasional drink at the local.

Edwina Anything else more — unusual?

David Oh, yes. Old cigarette cards. I've got an incredible collection. Thousands of them.

Edwina How interesting. The problem is, our young ladies prefer men with more — how shall I put it? — exotic pastimes. Now if you were into hang-gliding? Scuba-diving? Alpine skiing? No?

David I work — how shall I put it — unsociable hours.

Edwina That can be a problem. And leads neatly to the next question: your occupation?

David Journalist.

Jonathan Oh-oh!

Edwina *Off*-duty, I trust?

David *On*-duty, I regret to inform you. (*He presents a card*) My card.

Edwina Out!

David Sorry?

Edwina Get out of this office now! How dare you pretend ——

David I didn't pretend. You just assumed.

Edwina You hoodwinked me! Typical of the gutter press!

David I only wanted to ask ——

Edwina I'm not talking to any newspaper!

Jonathan Why not? *I've* got nothing to hide.

Edwina Well, I ha—— (*she checks herself. Snapping back at David*) I told you! On your way!

David OK. If that's the way you want it.

Edwina It is! And don't come back!

David Fine. It would have been fairer to hear your side, but I guess I'll have to base my article on what other people have told me.

Edwina Article? What article?

David (*moving to the door*) You can read all about it in next week's paper.

Edwina Wait! Just a minute.

David But I'm going like you told me to.

Edwina Don't — please? Look, Mr Murray — David — perhaps I did fly off the handle the teeniest bit, but you were naughty not telling us who you were at the beginning.

David Would you have let me in if you had known?

Edwina Of course. We've absolutely nothing to hide.

Jonathan (*enjoying all this*) Not much.

Edwina (*to Jonathan*) Button it! (*To David*) Do sit down.

David sits again

That's better. This article you mentioned?

David Just a little investigative piece about the dating business. Personal ads, computer dating, solo clubs, introduction agencies ... all that sort of stuff.

Jonathan (*looking at David's card*) Good old "human interest"?

David Right.

Jonathan Makes a nice change for your rag. Usually it's "I was a Homicidal Maniac's Mistress" or "Sex in the Convent: a Mother Superior Confesses".

Edwina You do realize we're not the only introduction agency?

David I do, but the editor chose yours especially.

Edwina Did he? Tell me, what did we have that all the others haven't?

David More complaints.

Edwina What?

David If people have a ruined holiday or buy a faulty second-hand car, who do they write to?

Jonathan The good old sensation-seeking tabloids.

David Right.

Edwina Complaints? Against us? Nonsense. I don't believe you.

Jonathan (*nudging the wastepaper bin aside with his foot*) You won't find one single letter of complaint in our files.

Edwina So, people grumble. It's a national pastime. But you papers never publish letters from all the satisfied customers. Oh, no. No muck for you there. (*She takes a folder of letters from the filing cabinet*) How about these? Go on. Pick any letter at random.

David (*selecting two letters*) OK. (*Reading*) "Please take my name off your files since thanks to your tireless efforts I have met my perfect partner." (*Reading the second letter*) "Heartfelt thanks for introducing me to the girl of my dreams." Yes, very impressive ... (*He compares the two letters*) But isn't the handwriting a bit similar?

Edwina (*snatching the letters back*) Rubbish. And what about these? (*She indicates the wedding photographs on the wall*) Indisputable proof.

David (*examining the photographs*) Ah, yes, yes. Those hairstyles of the sixties don't half look quaint now. And do you hire out wedding guests as well?

Edwina What do you mean?

David Most of the guests in this one turn up in this one — and that one.

Edwina Mere coincidence. All right, so we do get the occasional dissatisified customer. What business doesn't?

David (*thumbing through several pages of his notebook*) Occasional?

Edwina Matching people isn't just a matter of finding compatible interests. You've got the human factor. She's immaculately groomed. He looks like he's been dragged backwards through a hedge. He's a party-goer. She's a party-pooper. She wants commitment. He wants to play around. You get my point? Now, take Jonathan and I ——

David Yes. Can we dispense with that little pretence?

Edwina Pretence?

David (*consulting his notebook*) Like any good journalist, I've been doing my homework. According to my research, this business is registered under the names of *John*, not Jonathan, and *Edna*, not Edwina, *Crummy*.

Jonathan With an "e", if you please.

Edwina So? What can you do with a name like Crummey?

David Even with an "e"? Not much. But "Lovelock"? I ask you — "Lovelock"?

Edwina Why not? I'll bet half your famous romantic novelists have pseudonyms.

Jonathan (*mischievously*) And the rest'll have pen names.

Edwina (*ignoring him*) I thought "Lovelock" created a certain ambience.

David Spoiled the minute you walk in here. (*He checks the notebook*) Then there's a certain divorce case at the County Court next Tuesday.

Edwina My, we have been a busy little muck-raker.

David Just doing my job. Adultery, a little bird told me. Out of curiosity — and this won't go into print, Scout's honour — who's the guilty party?

Edwina and Jonathan point at each other

David Ah. Pity I'm covering the union conference next week.

Edwina So, Mr Ace Reporter, divorce is another crime in your eyes? Then half the people in this file are just as guilty. Oh, we get them all, from the shell-shocked "How could he do this to me?", to the men whose wives "didn't understand them", not to mention the ones who fancied a bit on the side and came a cropper.

David So that's half your customers. What about the rest?

Edwina The rest? Oh, yes. You think *we're* chancers? You should meet the ones we get. The blokes who think any woman who joins an agency must be desperate for "it", or those ladies who measure a gent by the size of his bank balance.

David No, I meant the — I suppose it's old fashioned to call them bachelors and spinsters.

Jonathan Singles. It sounds deceptively cheerful.

David The "singles" then. When do you break sweat for them, except when you rush to the bank with their cheques?

Edwina We try. But we can only do so much.

David Try to con them, you mean.

Edwina Look! Nobody twists their arms. I'll tell you why they come here.

Jonathan Because they haven't a hope in hell otherwise.

Edwina Exactly. Some of the people in this file you could strand on a desert island with someone of the opposite sex, and they still wouldn't make it.

David How?

Edwina How? If you haven't got what it takes, you haven't got it. Don't you believe all that poor lonely hearts rubbish. Excuses galore for not finding Mr or Miss Right.

David (*scribbling furiously*) This is getting interesting. Give me an example then.

Edwina Right. How about physical appearance for a start?

David Looks aren't everything.

Edwina I wish I had a fiver every time I heard that one. Of course they are! You've got to fancy the other person. Be honest, could you live with someone you couldn't stand the sight of?

Jonathan It has been known ...

David People can't help the way they were born.

Edwina No, but if they neglect their appearance, that's self-inflicted. (*She glances at Jonathan*) A man doesn't have to go to seed. (*She preens herself*) And a women has cosmetics.

Jonathan I've always said, if a woman has the looks, she doesn't need the make-up. And if she hasn't got the looks, she can paint her face until Doomsday, but ——

Edwina Thank you, Max Factor.

David Anything else they "haven't got"?

Edwina Personality. The social turkeys whose conversation make the speaking clock sound more interesting, or the crashing bores whose favourite topic is themselves.

David So, you're telling me nobody's genuine?

Edwina No, the sad thing is, most of them are, deep down.

David But if I had been a real customer, I'd have been wasting my time, wouldn't I?

Edwina Since I can't imagine a nice-looking bloke like yourself having any trouble finding a girlfriend, your question's academic.

David I do all right, thank you.

Edwina Pleased to hear it. Especially since you work ... (*she checks the form she filled in earlier*) "unsocial hours". You're lucky to have such an understanding girlfriend.

David (*unaware he has fallen into her trap*) Well — I'm not into anything serious at the moment.

Edwina (*realizing she has found an opening*) I see. Sort of — playing the field?

David That's right.

Edwina And you're young enough yet.

David Plenty of time. I do OK. But if I didn't, you wouldn't catch me in a place like this.

Jonathan Yet, here you are.

David Doing my job!

Edwina But why are you so interested in the dating business? What's your angle?

David Curiosity. Nothing else. I wondered what types ... Just what are you getting at?

Edwina Nothing.

David That's OK then.

Edwina I wasn't for one moment suggesting that your presence was prompted by your lack of a close, satisfying relationship. Not at all.

David I should think not! I told you, I do all right.

Edwina Of course you do.

David There's nothing lacking in my social life. It's very ...

Jonathan Busy?

David Yes ...

Edwina Rewarding?

David Most of the time.

Edwina Yes, after all ... (*She checks the form*) You've got your ten-pin bowling.

Jonathan Don't forget the cigarette cards.

Edwina How could I forget them? I'll bet they draw the girls. What a conversation stopper at parties.

David Well, I'm not really the party type.

Edwina No. But lots of girls must go to the ten-pin bowling?

David Lots. But they're always already attached.

Edwina I wish I'd another fiver for every time I hear that one as well.

David A fiver! Fifty quid you rip people off!

Jonathan What price happiness?

David I wouldn't pay your price. I'll find someone, sooner or later.

Edwina Could be later.

David I'll wait.

Edwina But until then?

David I'll survive.

Edwina In your empty flat.

Jonathan Trying not to talk to yourself.

Edwina Hoping maybe the phone will ring.

David Hang on! Wait a minute! I see what you're up to.

Edwina (*all innocence*) "Up to", David?

David Trying to make me feel bad about being on my own so you can justify making a fast buck.

Edwina Does this office look like the fruit of lots of fast bucks? I'm telling you, I practically run this as a charity.

Jonathan Bless you, Saint Edna.

Edwina And you did admit you are lonely.

David I did nothing of the kind!

Edwina So life's a bed of roses?

David I didn't say that! Life can be rotten on your own. It can get you down. So you just pick yourself up again. I've got friends. Mates I can go to the pub with.

Edwina Good for you. But I'll bet they've all got girlfriends.

David Most of them ... (*He thinks for a moment*) Hang on! *I'm* the one who's supposed to be asking *you* the questions.

Edwina I think you know your answer.

There is a polite knock at the door

Jonathan Hark! Who knocks at this untimely hour?

Edwina Who the hell is it now?

Jonathan Edna Crummey, humanitarian, matchmaker, bringer-together of countless happy couples, this is your life.

Edwina Just see who it is.

Jonathan opens the door

Susan Carter, a strikingly attractive girl, is standing outside

(*Shortly*) Yes?

Susan I'm looking for "Perfect Partners".

Jonathan Aren't we all?

Edwina You have the right place, but we are rather busy.

Susan I could come back some other time.

Jonathan Wouldn't dream of it. Do come in. I'm sure we can squeeze you in.

Jonathan ushers Susan in and closes the door. Edwina registers annoyance at this

Pray be seated.
David (*quickly getting a chair and placing it near his own*) Allow me.

Edwina and Jonathan exchange looks

Susan Thanks. (*She sits*)
Jonathan After all, here's an opportunity for the gentleman of the press to see how we usually conduct business.
Susan (*slightly alarmed*) Press? You mean newspapers?
David Don't worry. I'm only here getting some background for an article.
Susan I don't want my name in the papers.
Jonathan You're not the only one.
David It won't be. Confidentiality will be respected, Miss ——?
Susan Carter. Susan Carter.
David Hallo, Susan. I'm David, David Murray.
Edwina And I'm the Queen of Sheba and this is Solomon. And we have a business to run.
Susan Sorry. I only wanted to enquire about your service.
Edwina (*softening with the prospect of business*) Did you? Jolly good. In that case, I'll just give you one of our application forms to peruse. (*She hands Susan a form*)
Susan Right. Thanks.
David If I were you, I'd throw that away.
Susan Sorry?
Edwina She's not you, Clark Kent, so shut it! (*Back to Susan; charmingly*) Now, Miss Carter — Susan — if that's OK? Informality is our keyword, Susan. Let me explain how we go about things.
David I'll tell you, quicker than her. First, you fill out that form. Second, you fork out fifty quid. Third, she goes through her file of no-hopers who only have one thing in common: they're all being swindled.

Susan Swindled?

David That's right. Judging by the complaints my paper gets, would-be perfect partners are as well matched as — (*he searches for names*) Florence Nightingale and Rasputin.

Jonathan We should be so lucky to get a client as classy as Rasputin.

Edwina Now, just you listen ...

David No, you listen! If I had my way, I'd outlaw anybody and anything that profits from lonely people.

Edwina A crusader as well, are we?

David I'd ban porn magazines, blue movies, those "dial me and talk dirty" phone lines. I'd sweep the whole lot into the gutter where they belong.

Jonathan Says someone who works for the gutter press.

Edwina Look, Mr Murray ——

Jonathan Whatever happened to "David"?

Edwina I'm being serious here! (*To David*) Yes, all the porn does exist. We exist. And here's your journalistic "bottom line": we all exist because we're needed.

David No! I can't — I won't — accept that.

Edwina So, as the saying goes: print and be damned!

David I will! Don't you worry!

Edwina I'm not.

David Watch what happens to your business.

Edwina Nothing will happen. Let me put it this way: if you were drowning, would you ignore the only lifebelt in reach?

David I'd sooner drown.

Edwina Would you?

There is a reflective pause

Susan Hallo? Remember me? I'm the one who came in ten minutes ago.

Jonathan Of course. How could we forget someone so ——

David Look, I'm sorry you walked into all this. If you don't mind me saying so, you don't look like the sort of person who'd need to resort to ... I mean, with your looks ...

Susan Thanks for the compliment, Mr Murray.

David Please, call me David.

Susan OK, David.

Jonathan Why not? Informality is our keyword.

Susan I've got to be really honest and admit I'm here under false pretences.

Edwina Oh, no! She's got a microphone hidden in her bag.

Susan No, nothing like that. I've really come on behalf of a girlfriend. She's a single parent and doesn't get out much. I thought an agency might be the answer. She did try placing a personal ad in the paper.

David Did she meet lots of men?

Susan Yes. Married ones.

David That's interesting. Look, I'm still gathering material for my article. Perhaps you could tell me more about your friend's experiences. No names mentioned, of course. Tell you what, there's quite a decent pub just across the road ...

Jonathan Personally recommended.

David I wondered, perhaps, if you'd care to join me for a drink. We could have a chat — about your friend.

Susan That would be nice.

David Great!

Susan But ... I'm meeting my boyfriend — (*she glances at her watch*) and I'm going to be late. Some other time, perhaps?

David Sure.

Susan (*returning the application form to Edwina*) I don't think this'll be ideal for my friend. My worst enemy, maybe. It's been an education. Goodbye.

Jonathan opens the door for Susan

Susan exits

David Bye.

Edwina While goodbyes are lingering in the air ...

David Interview over?

Edwina Correct. (*As she is about to put the form back, she has second thoughts*) No use putting this away. (*She hands the form to him*) I'm sure you could use it.

David What for?

Edwina Research?

David Yes. If you think for one moment I'd ever ——

Edwina You never know, do you? Think about it next time you're sorting out your cigarette cards. Lots of young ladies in this file could be just right for you. We'd be happy to fix you up, gratis. (*She picks out the most dog-eared card of the lot*) Now, if you happened to like pets like, say, an Afghan hound?

David looks at the form, crushes it in his hand and drops it on the floor

David quietly exits without another word

Jonathan (*picking up the whisky bottle*) Can I tempt you?

Edwina This time, yes.

Jonathan empties the dregs of the bottle into two plastic cups and hands one to Edwina

Jonathan Here's to fame.

Edwina And infamy. Who cares what that rag prints? Half its readers can't read and the other half look at nothing between page three and the football reports.

Jonathan True. However, the time is nigh for another goodbye. (*He tosses the empty whisky bottle back into the filing cabinet*) Something to remember me by.

Edwina Do you have to go? Stay a bit.

Jonathan What for?

Edwina (*shrugging*) Just need to talk.

Jonathan Must fly, my darling. Never mind. You'll see me next Tuesday.

Edwina Hmmm?

Jonathan In court.

Jonathan departs

Edwina drains her whisky and throws the plastic cup into the bin. She sits for a while, looking thoroughly depressed. The phone rings. Edwina sighs and looks at the phone before answering it with somewhat less than her usual flair

Edwina Hallo. Yes? ... Yes, this is "Perfect Partners". ... You'd like to join. OK. Hold on. (*She gets another application form*) If I can just take down your particulars. ... Pardon? ... (*Humourlessly*) Oh, very funny. Can we start with your name? ... Mr Smith. ... Oh, yes. Age? ... Just turned fifty. ... (*To herself*) Fifty-five. ... (*Into the phone*) What's that? ... Friends say you don't look a day over forty. ... Oh, yes. ... I'm sure you don't. ... Address? ... Nice. Occupation? ... Company director. (*She brightens considerably*) Very nice. Interests? ... Expensive restaurants, fast cars, foreign travel. Extremely nice. ... Yes, I'm certain we can find your perfect partner. In fact, someone springs immediately to mind. (*She preens herself*) How would you like to meet an attractive, charming, sophisticated lady? ... What does she look like? You won't believe your luck. She's ... (*The actress playing the part describes herself; needless to say with embellishments, slight exaggerations and tactful omissions galore!*) How old? Oh, youthful forty — (*clearing her throat*) ahem! What's that? ... You'd prefer someone less mature. ... I see. ... Well, let's get our KN five-o-five digital computer to select your perfect partner. (*She switches on the cassette recorder and tackles the card file*) Ah, yes. Here we are. (*She switches off the recorder*) The very girl for you. Especially if you're fond of large dogs. ... No? ... You prefer hamsters. ... Right. Let's see who else we've got. (*She switches on the cassette recorder and continues thumbing through the card file*)

The Lights fade to Black-out

CURTAIN

FURNITURE AND PROPERTY LIST

On stage: Old desk. *On it*: papers, files, index card file with cards, portable cassette recorder, old-style telephone
3 chairs
Large wastepaper bin overflowing with papers
Filing cabinet. *In it*: half-full bottle of whisky, blank application forms, folder with letters
Wedding photographs on walls
Pile of unopened mail comprising red telephone bill, three handwritten letters, complete application form with cheque attached
Old newspapers
Plastic cups
Unwashed milk bottles

Off stage: Two supermarket carrier bags containing shopping and checkout slip (**Edwina**)

Personal: **Edwina**: keys, pen
David: business card, notebook, pen

LIGHTING PLOT

Property fittings required: nil

Interior. The same scene throughout

To open: General lighting

No cues

EFFECTS PLOT

Printed by
THE KINGFISHER PRESS, LONDON NW10 6UG